Customer service
? and answers
PART 1

OTENG MONTSHITI

CUSTOMER SERVICE
? AND ANSWERS
PART 1
Copyright ©2018
CONTACT ADDRESS: OTENG MONTSHITI
P O BOX M1139
KANYE
BOTSWANA

E-MAIL ADDRESS:
otengmontshiti@gmail.com
Contact number: (+267) 74 644 954

Table of contents

Acknowledgement

I would like to thank my family for their support especially my lovely wife who supported me in writing this book.

Customer service
Questions and answers
Introduction

Champions are discovered during hard or trying times. Beyond every challenge there is promotion and breakthrough. If you don't like them you will never be celebrated in life and people who make it in life are always prepared for challenges. Before people become presidents they prepare themselves outside parliament not inside.

Students must be prepared for examination.

They must read their books and share knowledge and skills. No man can exist in isolation. The following can help them;

1. Draft timetables

2. Conduct researches because students who pass with highest grade read different books in that course. Read a chapter and answer question on that chapter from previous examinations this will prepare you for the environment of examination.

3. Students must trouble teachers by submitting assignments not vice verse because your future is in your hands and teachers are there to correct, teach and encourage you.

4. Form study groups

5.Identify your weakness and strengths. In examination begin with questions that you know you will pass with highest marks.

6. Mark your work before the examiners do the actual marking.

There is no marks for quantity but what gain marks is quality (accuracy, clear and well structured ideas)

7. Write as if the examiners don't know anything.

8. Be neat, correct spelling errors and avoid long sentences because they lose meaning.

9. Read your work atleast twice before you summit.

Key words in examination

Explain- to tell somebody about something in a way that makes it easy to understand

Mention/state/name/List- you write items one by one.

Discuss- to write about positive, negative and come up with recommendations

Define- you give the meaning of a word or phrase.

Identify- to recognize something and explain it in details.

Compare/Contrast-to differentiates between two things or more.

Elaborate/ illustrate- to explain something clearly and support your answer with diagrams or pictures.

Distinguish- to recognize the difference between two or more items.

NB Don't forget to give examples in the examination.

Answers

Follow instructions

Use your own words as much as possible because examiners test your understanding and application.

Your answers must have:

Introduction
1.. Should be short and specific.

2. It is used to explain key words or difficult words.

Body
1. Should start with topic
sentence which states the
main point of the paragraph

2. The rest of the paragraph
should expand or explain
the topic sentence.

Conclusion
1. It states the writer's point
of view or summaries the
whole passage

Discuss how customer service staff can be rewarded for excellent performance?

Rewards
1. Training
2. Trophies and medals
3. Hall of fame
4. Life insurance
5. Medical aid
6. Holidays
7. Vouchers Customer service does not come easily because it requires commitment from both customer service staff and managers.

One of the strategies to award customer service staff is to send them to prestigious universities to amass wide knowledge and skills. This will help them to do their job more confidently than never before..

For example, Debswana Diamond Mine in Botswana send it's employees on regular basis to upgrade their knowledge and skills at University of Botswana, Technical Colleges and even abroad at counties like Canada, United States of America to do Mining Engineering.

Customer service staff can be given trophies as rewards. This will keep them focused and create a competitive environment in the working place. For example, in World Wrestling Entertainment (WWE), entertainers (superstars) are given awards like the best match of the year.

The Hall of Fame is another thing that can be used to reward customer service staff. This award is usually given to employees who have worked for the company tirelessly and showed loyalty to the company.

For example, each year before WrestleMania matches in World Wrestling Entertainment, superstars who have been loyal to the company are awarded WWE Hall of Fame awards.

One of the strategies is to reward customer service staff is incentives like bonus. Most of the companies at the end of the year they give their employees some money as bonus. For example, mining companies give their employees double pay at the end of the year.

Companies can reward customer service staff with life insurance, accident cover and so forth. This will help the employees to focus on their job rather than worrying about who will take care of them if they are injured in the working place. They will have a peace of mind knowing that their lives are in good hands.

Companies can reward their customer service staff with voucher which can be redeemed anywhere or at specified outlets.

They can purchase groceries, clothes and other necessities. The company can state that it want its vouchers to be redeemed at Wal-Mart or Tesco if it is in United States of America or Britain.

There are times when companies reward the customer service staff with the opportunity to go on holiday or visit historic sites like Okavango Delta, The Great Wall of China and so forth. This privilege is usually given to the best employees.

Customer service staff should be rewarded at all times as a token of saying thank you. This will motivate them to work harder and ultimately the company will prosper.

How is technology changing customer service provision in the twenty first century? (ICM, MAY 2013)

Customers in the twenty first century are demanding and sophisticated at the same time. They are exposed to so many information e.g. on Facebook, internet, billboards etc. They are not loyal because they have wide variety of goods and services to choose from. They don't forgive easily if you harm their feelings they boycott your business and go somewhere else. But thanks! Be to technology which has changed everything and make life easier for both customer service provider and customers.

Today powerful companies like American computer manufacturing company Dell allows customers to design or give specification of the computer they want. This includes colors, hard drive, RAM and the speed of the processor. The company will manufacture a computer for such a customer.

Technology has destroyed the roles of the middle men like wholesalers and retailers. Companies can address and meet customer needs directly.

Today International Examination Bodies like Institute of Commercial Management (ICM), The Association of Business Executive (ABE) no longer give study materials to colleges and universities rather they drop items directly in the students' electronic accounts or email.

This has helped ICM to serve students fast and improve their customer service.

Customers no longer go to companies and join long line to pay for water or electricity. Customers just need a mobile phone to purchase electricity and to send money electronically from one company to the next. For example, Botswana Unified Revenue Service (BURS) business people can pay tax man online at the comfort of their homes.

The role of bush mechanic and garages will be affected terrible. They will lose their business or close down totally because today customers can access internet, type the model, specify the problem and the manufacturer on-line trouble shooting programme will give the answer or solution.

Currency conversion-today because of advanced and sophisticated technology Automated Teller Machines can change Rand to Pula and vice versa.

This has saved and made life of customer easier. They no longer line up at the banks to receive service. Technology in the area of call centers cannot be overlooked. Companies offer free hot line which are available 24 hours, 7 days a week. Some companies websites offer free call me facilities.

This encourages customers to call and make suggestions, complaints, comments and complements. This has helped companies to provide excellent customer service.

Technology has changed the world and turned it into a global village. Goods and services can be purchased from America while a customer is in Botswana. For example, customers can purchase books from Amazon online at 5 dollars and in two weeks it will be here in Botswana. Technology has enhanced customer service in a positive way.

What are the FIVE basic needs of every customer? (1CM, MARCH 2013)

Whether a company is selling products like retail shops or providing service like banking, insurance and so forth customers expect the five basic needs to be available. Otherwise they will be dissatisfied and take business to your rivals or competitors. These five basic needs of every customer are;

1. Price
2. Quality
3. Service

4. Appreciation
5. Action

1. PRICE

If the demand is high the price becomes high. If the market is saturated then the price of the product or service becomes cheaper. For example, if the numbers of hotels in Gaborone the capital city of Botswana are increasing at a rapid speed then hotel companies are forced to lower prices because customers have wider range of choices.

In marketplace whereby a single company dominates the market (monopoly) the prices are usually higher because customers have no other options. For example, Botswana Power Corporation is the only company at sells electricity in Botswana.

2. QUALITY

When customers buy a product they look at the quality. If the quality is low they take business to your rivals. If the quality of goods and services are high the prices are high. For example, BMW is very expensive because this brand manufactures products of highest quality, safety and speed.

3. ACTION

Customers want to be assured that when products are not working they can be assisted. If the products are not working or have questions they can ask at anytime. For example, most companies offer toll free numbers to assist customers 24 hours using excellent customer service staff. Today because of technology, when customers are having problems with products they just get online troubleshooting programs and fix the problem or get refunded.

4. APPRECIATION

Customers want to be appreciated at all times. Shop assistants must smile and say "thank you". Companies write on the receipts "Thank you call again". There are times when big companies write "thank you for shopping at Montshiti Holdings". This is very important because customers have chosen you not your rivals.

5. SERVICE

Either you are selling a product or service, an excellent service should be offered.

People must be available to help you as a customer like shop assistants even if it is self service. Someone must be available to be asked if customers don't find something in the shop. That person must be trustworthy not the situation whereby security officers steal customers products.

Why is customer service so rare? (1CM, MARCH 2013)

You state the reasons and explain them deeper

Excellent customer service is rare because companies just want to reap, harvest. There is a simple rule in this world you reap what you have sown. When companies are supposed to plant (invest)in customer service they are reluctant to do so. This is what excellent customer service requires;

1. Spending money
2. Training

1. SPENDING

Marketing and customer service relies heavily on regular research. Therefore customer service providers should conduct market research to evaluate their strength and weakness. The most important thing in business is to turn your weakness into strength. Powerful companies like Coca Cola conduct market research on continuous basis. This is done to help the company to come up with strategies or ways to meet customers changing needs and wants.

Customers needs and wants keep on changing on regular basis. If you don't keep up with them you will offer wrong products and service to your customers. If this materializes customers will boycott your company and go elsewhere. Conducting a market research is not easy as it sounds. It requires recruiting relevant people, where possible lure customers to participate by offering free snacks and other relevant resources like papers, cars and laptops. These people must go through vigorous training to be competent and produce what is required.

2. TRAINING

Excellent customer service doesn't come easily. It requires skills, experience and knowledge in the field of customer service. It requires personal and interpersonal skills otherwise conflicts will be in the order of the day in your company. One of the requirements is to emphasize with customers. This means putting yourself as customer service provider on the shoes of your customers.

This will help the customer service provider to treat customers the way he or she wants to be treated.

For example, British Airways has trained its employees like pilots to smile at customers at all times. They are taught the techniques of handling microphone. This has made British Airways one of the best in the world.

Now then, companies should let these facts sink in their minds and come up with policies that encourages the training of employees and should be ready to invest in customer service. Otherwise you can't reap where you haven't sown. This involve evaluating the skills and knowledge of your employees through regular survey to see if they are ready or equipped with rightful skills and knowledge to solve customer's problems professionally.

Explain what you understand by the term reputation management? (1CM, JUNE 2013)

Reputation management is how customers think or perceive your company as opposed to image management which deals with how the company would like to be perceived by customers. It is not the some thing that comes easily. It requires identifying how the company is viewed and come up with an action plan to correct, maintain or enhance the company's reputation.

For example, a company can have powerful image or brand but having poor reputation. It can sell goods of poor quality, pay employees poorly (bad reputation) but selling at lower prices as compared to its competitors making huge profits (powerful brand).

Companies must conduct market research on regular basis to measure their level of reputation. This will help companies to identify their strength and weakness. They can now turn their weakness into strength and come up with strategies to maintain their strength.

It is very surprising, there are times when a company is liked by the community in which it's operating in but customers may take business elsewhere. If your company has good reputation it should maintain that realm. Otherwise that brand is automatically programmed to fail. If it is a bad reputation it should be corrected using public relation strategies. For example, Johnson and Johnson scandal it happened that one of their product 3 killed. Its brand was viewed by people in the bad light. Public relation strategies were used to correct the error and it came back as one of the powerful brand in the mind of consumers.

Company with good reputation is very responsive to customers. It responds quickly to customer comments, enquiries or problems and come up with creative solutions. Goods and service well on time, It delivers goods and services well in time, provides guarantee and warranties and make regular follow ups.

Company with good reputation is very progressive in terms of technology. It introduces electronic wallet (e-wallet), electronic banking whereby customers deposit cash using the Automatic Teller Machines (ATM). In this modern era advanced and sophisticated technology allows customers to change Botswana Pula to South African Rand using ATM.

Companies with good reputation have strong financial performance. They usually publish their shares at Stock Exchange. We can think of the world wealthiest man Mr Bill Gates' powerful company known as Microsoft which has been listed at American Stock Exchange. It publishes its financial statements on regular basis.

Companies with good reputation are a good citizens. It simply means they give back to the community. This can be done through housing and caring for less privileged people,

people living with disability,
widows and widowers and so forth. It also sponsors sporting activities e.g. Sony and Heineken are proud sponsors of UEFA championships. Coca Cola sponsors world cup a foot ball event.

Companies with good reputation are honest. It doesn't get tenders by dishonest means like bribery or corruption. It follows appropriate channels.

In simple terms, if the reputation of the company is not

maintained in positive light the results can be very dangerous. That is why powerful brands like Coca Cola have powerful reputation across the world.

Discuss the barriers to excellent customer service? (1CM, MAY 2013)

Excellent customer service is not cheap talk it is too costly. It doesn't come easily. It comes with barriers or challenges. They are part of life and no one can avoid them. These barriers are in two categories namely;

1. Barriers which are under the control of the service provider
2. Barriers which are beyond the control of the service provider.

One of those barriers that are under the control of the service provider is laziness. This is not only disgusting but can destroy business. This occurs if internal customers or employees take long to help customers or drag their feet in the working place. They must show willingness to work and corporate with customers. The best recommendation is to encourage customer service provider to be active and exercise on regular interval to keep their body fit every day.

The other barrier is

moodiness. This is whereby today the customer service provider is smiling and happy the next day he or she is not. This can chase customers away. The recommendation is to teach employees to put their personal issues behind them in the working place and act professionally.

Insufficient authority is another barrier. It is whereby everyone does what he or she wants. The rules and regulations are not observed. The likely recommendation is to enforce laws and regulations to avoid the situation whereby everything gets out of control.

Understaffing and overstaffing is another barrier. If the company is under staffed there will be few people doing many tasks. If it is overstaffed there will be too many people doing less work. The likely recommendation is to employ the right number of personnel for the job.

The other barrier is language. This is common in Botswana where customers mostly speak Setswana and English. It is difficult to communicate with the Chinese. The likely recommendation is to enroll with universities offering Chinese courses today.

Other barriers are beyond the control of customer service providers like laws. Laws can be an obstacle. For example, in Botswana all bars open at 2 pm and close mid night during weekends. There is nothing customer service provider can do but the best way is close down business to to avoid heavy penalties.

The other barrier is restrictive policies of the organization. This is common armed forces like police and army. This doesn't allow employees to be creative but to be shallow minded. The likely recommendation is to let customer service provider to be creative by empowering them in the working place.

These barriers must be recognized at all times and customer service provider should be equipped with knowledge and skills to overcome them. This will help them to tackle various situations or challenges.

Discuss the costs of losing a customer?

Customer service is a tool that a business can use to destroy its competitors. It simply means addressing the needs and wants of customers. If customer service is not provided customers will take business to your competitors and bring the following consequences on the scene:

1. Loss of business
2. Loss of jobs
3. Loss of reputation

4. Loss of money

1. LOSS OF BUSINESS

If you don't offer excellent customer service you are going to lose your business to your competitors. Customer service providers must know that they are not the only people in the marketing place. For example if customers are buying from so and so company and employees are rude they will go to another company offering excellent customer service.

2. LOSS OF EMPLOYMENT

When there is no business

automatically the company will be forced to terminate the employment contract of their workers to reduce costs. Therefore, it will be disastrous in the business sense because the company will be forced to close down all unprofitable outlets.

3. LOSS OF REPUTATION

The word of mouth is very dangerous weapon in the hands of customers. It has power to build and destroy. If customers are not happy they will talk negatively about you therefore degrading your reputation.

For example, Johnson and Johnson faced a trying time some years ago when their product killed some people. They have to use public relations strategies to correct the error and rebuild their reputation.

4. LOSS OF MONEY

Automatically when customers lose trust in you as a customer service provider they take their money somewhere or to your competitors to be precise.

Money makes the world go round.

There will be no money to pay employees, pay expenses like water, electricity etc. and ultimately the business will close down.

The cost of losing a customer is totally big and can have huge financial impact on the day to day running of the business. The cost of losing a loyal customer is beyond assessment.

Explain how you might plan to exceed customer expectations.

Customer service is not something you wake up one morning and start practicing it. Excellent customer service must be planned thoroughly to exceed your customer expectations. The following techniques are useful;

As customer service provider you have to know your customers needs and wants deeply. You have to know their buying patterns; why they buy from you, what product they usually buy, does your customer buy during month end special or fortnightly. It is wrong to treat your customers as a group You have to treat them as individuals. For example, an accountant needs and wants are different from the herd boy's from the cattle post.

It is always best to know what customers expect from you. This should be done on continuous basis through market research. For example, you have to ask them how many minutes they expect to wait for the assistance to be available.

As a customer service provider you should be in a position to tell your customer what they can expect. This must be done looking at infrastructures like telephone lines, technology available like internet and scanner system.

As customer service provider it is a must for you to deliver what you have promised customers. Be a person who fulfills his or her promises to customers.

Otherwise they will go to competitors. For example, if you tell customers that every week of the end of the month is special but when they arrive at your business it is not there. It is wrong.

Maintain the same standard of excellent customer service. In similar situations treat them the same way. For example, if your shop is clean today and tidy then the next day it is dirty it is wrong.

Customer service provider has to know which method(s)

is best for the business to
use. They can use electronic
mail, fax machines and
many others. It will depend
on the customers'
knowledge and skills. For
example, if your customers
have got internet
connectivity at home you
can use email to
communicate with them.

List example of customer service?

a. on time delivery
b. well explained instructions
c. easy to use website
d. calling customers by names
e. smiling at your customer at all times

Why is customer retention important?

Customer retention is whereby the company tries on continuous basis to satisfy and maintain current customers in business. Plan must be in place to achieve it. If it is done in disorderly manner it is very destructive to the survival of the business.

1. Internal customers
It is better to retain people working in the business because it is much costly to train and induct new employees.

High labor turn over will result if internal customers are not taken care of. If they are taken care of they will give testimonials because of loyalty to the company.

2. External customers
It is better to keep old customers rather than new ones because it requires high advertising and promotion. A customer is always a customer even if he or she doesn't want anything e.g. doing window shopping.

There should be follow-ups to see if the product is working or not.

There should be after service delivery- free repair of the product.

For example; salons now wash hair for free and that is going beyond customer expectations.
NOTES: our relationship with customers is for long life.

Define;

1. Customer satisfaction
It measures how well the product or service of the company meet customer expectations. If the quality of goods or service, the location (accessibility), the environment within the organization doesn't meet customers' expectations they will be dissatisfied and take business elsewhere. Customer satisfaction must be measured on regular intervals using customer survey.

2. Segmentation

It is dividing or breaking down of customers into groups of similar needs and wants. It helps the companies to know how many existing customers are there, how much they spend, when they buy e.g. end of month specials and which group of customers generate profit.

It is not very segment that is profitable. The company must focus on profitable segments and ignore non-profitable ones. This can be achieved if regular market research is conducted on regular basis because customers preference and tastes keep on changing.

3. Demand
It is the desire for a product or service backed up with money and willingness to pay. For example, if you want to buy a car and you don't have money to pay for it then there is no demand.

Discuss the importance of providing a good service to internal customers?

Internal customers are people who are working in the company. Departments can be customers to another department e.g. at the end of each financial all department s submit their financial statements to the Account department. In this way other departments are customers of the Accounting Department. Internal customers are very important to the success and prosperity of your business.

If internal customers are happy they will produce goods and service of highest quality using available resources. This minimizes wastage. They provide goods which meet needs and wants of customers not what the company can produce because customers are not satisfied as a group. They are satisfied on individual basis because they have different tastes and preferences.

If internal customers are satisfied there will be no absenteeism because employees will be motivated and encouraged every day to come to work well on time and prepared for the day. Some companies offer their employees with free tea break and lunch.

If top management consults them on regular basis they will be satisfied. They will work as if the company belongs to them. This means there will be productivity in the working place. Internal customers will say, "Our goals not top management goal".in simple words, they will not distance themselves from challenges when come across your path because they participated in decision making.

It is important to provide good customer service to internal customers because they are people who interact with customers on daily basis. Therefore, they know their needs and wants better. If they are not given the respect and honor they deserve they will not share valuable information to customer as a way of punishing you.

If internal customers are not treated very

nicely they will tarnish the image of the company. They are brand ambassadors. When the company wants skilled person internal customers will recommend or tell their families and friends to apply for the position but if they are dissatisfied they will discourage them.

Internal customers are important because they can become loyal to the company and work for many years. This saves money because it is very expensive to recruit new employees. They have to go

under vigorous training and
training is costly.

The importance of internal
customers cannot be
overlooked by companies
today. If the management
treats them nicely the
business will prosper.

Lightning Source UK Ltd.
Milton Keynes UK
UKHW020803160119
335572UK00015B/2083/P